CRAFTY FAST FOOD

Michael Barry
and Oz Clarke

Photographs by Gus Filgate

BBC BOOKS

I would like to thank my editor Anna Ottewill, the designer Isobel Gillan, and Alison Oakervee
who helped test and check the recipes, for their kindness, patience and skill.

This book is published to accompany the television series entitled *Food & Drink*
produced for BBC television by Bazal Productions
Executive Producer: Peter Bazalgette
Producer: Tim Hincks

Published by BBC Books,
an imprint of BBC Worldwide Ltd.,
Woodlands, 80 Wood Lane, London W12 0TT

First published 1998
© Crafty Cooking Limited, Oz Clarke and Bazal Productions Limited
Photographs by Gus Filgate © BBC Books

ISBN: 0 563 38410 7

Commissioning Editor: Anna Ottewill
Art Director: Frank Phillips
Copy Editor: Susannah Tee
Designer: Isobel Gillan
Recipe tester: Alison Oakervee
Home Economist: Carol Tennant
Stylist: Penny Markham
Illustrator: Kate Simunek

Typeset by BBC Books in Gill Sans
Printed by Cambus Litho Limited, East Kilbride, Scotland
Binding by Hunter and Foulis Limited, Edinburgh, Scotland
PPC and jacket printed by Lawrence Allen Limited, Weston-super-Mare
Colour reproduction by Radstock Reproductions Limited, Midsomer Norton, Bath

Photograph on page 2: Ice-cream toppings *(clockwise from the left):* Hot Banana Toffee *(see p. 166),*
Cheat's Chocolate Sauce *(see p. 164),* Butterscotch Pistachio Sauce *(see p. 165)*
and Raspberry Coulis *(see p. 162).*

Contents

Introduction

I have a confession to make. I love shopping, particularly in supermarkets. It's not the compulsion to spend necessarily. I can browse in a supermarket for up to an hour, particularly a well-stocked one, and only come away with two or three items. There are two reasons why I'm such a great fan of them. One is that they carry a wider range of products (some of the larger ones up to 15,000 separate lines), and a greater choice of fresh produce than any other in the world. In individual countries, of course, you might find a better choice of certain specialized foods – a bigger range of frankfurters in an American supermarket, for example, or soft cheeses in a French one – but for overall variety we are almost certainly the world leaders. The other reason is that I'm an experimenter. I like trying new foods, new tastes, new flavours and new ways of doing things, and that's what our supermarkets are increasingly offering us.

On top of this vast choice of products, supermarkets are introducing more and more ready-made meals too. The range of ready-prepared dishes at some of our larger supermarkets is so enormous one could almost run an Indian restaurant with these meals alone.

But buying ready-prepared dishes is an expensive way to eat, and for those of us who like putting our own meals together, not a very satisfying one. So, if you enjoy cooking but find it almost impossible to fit it into your everyday life, the recipes in this book should be just what you're looking for. By taking advantage of the abundance of part-prepared convenience products in our supermarkets and cutting out time-consuming preparations back in the kitchen, all the dishes in this book can be made simply, inexpensively and most of all, in next to no time.

Take curries for example. You will find a huge choice of pre-prepared sauces, curry pastes, mixes, spices and powders on your supermarket shelves that will allow you to make your own Indian curries with speed and ease. You'll find vegetables too, washed, trimmed and ready for use, and herbs like coriander and mint, pre-packaged or growing in little pots, all for your convenience. To accompany your curry, you'll find many different kinds of Indian breads: naans, paratha and chapati. Then there'll be a variety of poppadoms to choose from and more kinds of mango chutney than I could possibly list here. And if you fancy making a cucumber salad to cool the mouth, you'll find at least five or six different kinds of plain yoghurt.

Crafty Fast Food is about taking advantage of these wonderful convenience products so that you can continue to cook your own meals as well as manage a busy lifestyle. Okay, sometimes, when you have the time or inclination, when you want to create your own special meal for family or friends, you might start with a whole head of garlic, grind it carefully to a paste, peel and finely-chop some ginger, blend five or six spices together in a mortar and pestle, and joint and bone a chicken before you even start cooking. But in the real world, and, for most of us, particularly during the week, that's not a realistic option and that's when the purées of ginger and garlic, ready-boned chickens and jars of well-blended masala paste come into their own, making it not only possible to make your own curry but to enjoy making it too rather than it being a lengthy chore at the end of a tiring day.

This leads on to the other main advantage of the recipes in this book: time. They can all be made in thirty minutes or under, and by that I mean total preparation and cooking time. This means that even a three-course meal, whether it be a simple family supper or posh dinner party, can be on the table in less than an hour.

Not only will you be able to cook your own food with speed and ease but you'll find your purse is vastly enhanced too. A recent test-run made on reicpes using crafty ingredients revealed that they cost less than half the price of the same ready-made alternatives. Fresh food, cooked by yourself, with the minimum of effort in under thirty minutes. Now that's what I call crafty cooking! Over to you Oz.

MICHAEL BARRY

Very crafty cooking indeed! Thank goodness it only takes a corkscrew to get inside a bottle of wine! Mind you, even that will get easier as more and more producers recognize the benefits of screw-tops!

Like Michael, I spend a lot of time browsing in the supermarket. But I'm rummaging amongst the wines – and there's some serious rummaging out there to do! At my last count, the top two supermarket giants each carried well over 600 different wines from some 25 different countries. Okay, so not every single branch stocks every single wine but these are awesome statistics nevertheless.

It's not surprising then, that the biggest bugbear I hear about is that the wine shelves are just too confusing and that no-one has the time to navigate their way through this formidable maze. Hang on, though. If you've left your wine shopping until last, you've probably been in the supermarket for ages already and can't wait to get out. The trolley is heavy and a pain to manoevre, the ice-cream is beginnning to melt and if you have a couple of screaming kids in tow as well…it's not surprising if you simply grab any old £2.99 multi-buy and make a fast escape to the checkout.

I think it's time to adopt a different strategy, to reach out and be more adventurous. Write 'wine' at the top of the shopping list and physically go to the wine aisles first. Do some homework before you set off for the supermarket. If you know you're going to try Michael's grilled salmon recipe, say, take a look at my wine suggestions to go with it and jot them down on your shopping list. Or, if you just fancy a wine change but don't know where to start, read my 'Lookalikes' section. Learn some label lore – every tiny scrap of knowledge helps. The wine shelves won't look so mysterious and threatening if you have a better idea of what you're looking for, you'll end up with more suitable and enjoyable wine and it will save you heaps of time, I promise.

Most supermarkets arrange wines by colour and by country of origin, broken down into various regions where appropriate. Some do things a little differently, though, adopting layouts based on wine style. There's also an admirable staff wine education initiative being taken by the supermarket bosses – the larger branches of most of the big supermarkets now have trained wine advisors on hand to offer assistance if you need it – and don't be afraid to ask! We're well out of the wine snob era and no-one is going to think you a fool for seeking advice. You wouldn't think twice about asking for it at the deli counter now, would you?

In-store wine tastings? I'm all for them! What a difference it can make when you're given the chance to taste before you buy. Back labels are getting better and better, too, and it's worth taking the trouble to read them as they're often packed full of useful information. Come to think of it, some of the front labels are pretty neat too – Great with Fish, Christmas Pudding Wine, Great with Michael Barry's *Crafty Fast Food*?! No, no – that's what I'm here for!

OZ CLARKE

Recipe Index by Ingredient

RECIPE INDEX BY INGREDIENT

12

STARTERS

SOUPS

You might ask yourself, 'Why bother to make soup from scratch or even from convenience ingredients when they're available in every form, from packet to fresh, chilled, ready-to-eat?' There are two or three answers. One is undoubtedly flavour. However well made the ready prepared soups are, they lack the intense flavour and richness of soups you prepare yourself. Economics also plays a part, for chilled soup, needed for more than two, costs quite a lot or requires several cans or packets. Last but not least is the issue of variety. Whatever one's childhood memories of canned tomato soup, there's no question that, once you've got past mushroom and chicken, even with today's attempts at dressing up alternative flavours, there is simply not enough variety. It's in these areas that I've tried to offer some choice here.

You'll find recipes from the Mediterranean such as *Red Pepper Roule Cheese Soup* or *Quick Italian Bean Soup,* and from Northern Europe, with a soup that's almost a stew, Lentil and Frankfurter. In all cases they're very easy to make, using ready prepared ingredients, but they have that distinctive home-made flavour of comfort and generosity.

Spinach and Chick Pea Soup

This is a soup with a Middle Eastern flavour and a very pleasant, slightly grainy texture. The combination of spinach and chick peas is extremely nutritious and, as it's so easy to make, it can be regularly included on the menu. Don't omit the lemon juice as it lifts the flavour of the soup quite dramatically.

time

25 mins

● Frozen spinach is an unusual product in that it's fine when used in dishes but not terribly satisfactory if served on its own as a vegetable, although there are some very expensive French frozen food shops which would strongly disagree with me.

● Dishes it is excellent in, as well as economical and easy to use, are soups and as a bed for sauces or meats such as *Chicken Florentine* (see p. 119).

Serves 4

2 tablespoons olive oil
1 large onion, finely chopped
420 g (14½ oz) can chick peas
250 g (9 oz) frozen spinach
salt and freshly ground black pepper
750 ml (1¼ pints) chicken stock
juice of 1 lemon

Heat the olive oil in a saucepan and gently fry the onion for about 5 minutes, until pale golden. Drain the chick peas into a sieve, rinse under cold water then stir the chick peas and spinach into the onions. Stir gently until the spinach wilts. Season generously with salt and pepper and add the chicken stock. Bring to the boil and simmer for 10 minutes. You can eat the soup as it is or, if preferred, purée it in a food processor. Before serving, stir in the lemon juice.

SOUPS

Spinach
CRAFTY INGREDIENT

Red Pepper and Roulé Cheese Soup Ⓥ

One of the most attractive of the processed cheeses that have emerged from France in recent years is the roulé. A mixture of creamy white soft cheese, garlic and green herbs, its spiral, catherine-wheel shape conceals how useful it can be in a variety of dishes. In this soup, mixed with the bright colours of red peppers, its pungency adds an unexpected creaminess and kick which combine to make a soup that is as delicious hot as it is cold.

time

25 mins

Serves 4

2 tablespoons olive oil

250 g (9 oz) onions, chopped

250 g (9 oz) potatoes, chopped

450 g (1 lb) red peppers, seeded and chopped

salt and freshly ground black pepper

750ml (1¼ pints) boiling water

100 g (4 oz) garlic and herb roulé cheese

1 tablespoon chopped fresh or frozen parsley, to garnish

Heat the oil in a large saucepan and fry the onions, potatoes and peppers for 4–5 minutes, until softened slightly. Season generously with salt and pepper, before pouring in the boiling water. Simmer for 10–12 minutes until the potatoes are cooked.

Pour half the mixture into a food processor and blend until smooth. Pour into a serving bowl. Add the remaining mixture and the roulé cheese to the food processor and blend until smooth. Stir the two mixtures together. Serve hot or cold, sprinkled with the parsley.

GARLIC AND HERB CHEESE (ROULE)

● While this cheese usually comes in a slice resembling a Swiss roll in shape, it can also be bought as a soft cheese mixed with garlic and herbs. They both taste very much the same although the Swiss roll version looks prettier.

● It's excellent spread on hamburgers and flashed under the grill for a rather tangy cheeseburger.

● Beaten with a little milk to make it soft and smooth, it makes a very good dip for crisps or raw vegetables.

Garlic and Herb Cheese

CRAFTY INGREDIENT

SOUPS

Quick Italian Bean Soup Ⓥ

Italian bean soups are famous, particularly in the region of Tuscany where the people are known as mangiafagioli *or bean-eaters. The soups come in a variety of styles and colours, according to the season, and minestrone is the name we give to just one of them. This soup tends to be an autumn or winter dish, designed to warm as well as nourish. It can be a meal in itself, eaten with good bread and followed by a little cheese and fruit.*

time

25 mins

Serves 4

420 g (14½ oz) can borlotti beans
4 tablespoons olive oil
1 large onion, thinly sliced
1 garlic clove, crushed
100 g (4 oz) carrots, diced
salt and freshly ground black pepper
1 litre (1¾ pints) water
100 g (4 oz) tomatoes, diced into 1 cm (½ inch) cubes
225 g (8 oz) cabbage, finely sliced
2 tablespoons Parmesan cheese, to serve

Drain the beans in a sieve and rinse under cold water. Heat the olive oil in a large saucepan and gently fry the onion and garlic for 3–4 minutes, until soft.

Stir in the carrots and continue to cook for a further 2–3 minutes, then add the beans. Season generously with salt and plenty of pepper before stirring in the water. Then simmer for 10 minutes.

Stir in the tomatoes and cabbage and bring to the boil. Simmer for a further 5 minutes, then serve sprinkled with Parmesan cheese.

CANNED BEANS

● These are available in a wide variety of shapes, sizes and flavours and are excellent as they not only save enormous amounts of time but are one of the few things that seem to be equally good whether canned or freshly cooked at home.

● You can use canned beans in soups, purées, mixed together with French dressing as a salad, or as a basis for one of the many traditional peasant bean dishes such as *Quick Chilli Con Carne* (see p. 79) from Mexico or Cassoulet from France.

Beans

CRAFTY INGREDIENT

Lentils
CRAFTY INGREDIENT

Lentil and Frankfurter Soup

This is not so much a soup as a stew really, and hugely nutritious, combining fibre as well as the protein of lentils with those delicious smoked sausages that we know as frankfurters. If possible, it's important to try and find the best ones you can and avoid the bright pink canned variety. I also think American-style beef frankfurters have the best flavour. These days it's also possible to find vegetarian frankfurters which work equally well in this soup. It's not, by any means, a first course to a meal but, on a cold winter's night, a big bowl is about the most warming thing I know.

time

30 mins

CANNED LENTILS

● Like beans, canned lentils are a great time saver because they need no soaking or prolonged cooking before use. Green lentils are quite substantial and don't turn into a mush like the more commonly known red lentils.

● The green ones make an excellent salad mixed with a good French dressing and perhaps some fresh vegetables such as spring onions and red peppers.

● They also make an excellent basis for the lentil and sausage dishes that abound in Middle Europe where the lentils are heated through in a little oil or fat and served as a bed for grilled sausages.

Serves 4

25 g (1 oz) butter
25 ml (1 fl oz) olive oil
250 g (9 oz) onions, grated
250 g (9 oz) potatoes, grated
250 g (9 oz) carrots, grated
420 g (14½ oz) can green or brown lentils
½ teaspoon turmeric
½ teaspoon chilli powder
salt and freshly ground black pepper
1.2 litres (2 pints) boiling water
350 g (12 oz) frankfurters
chopped fresh parsley, to garnish

Heat the butter and oil in a large saucepan and gently fry the onions, potatoes and carrots. Meanwhile, drain the lentils into a sieve and rinse well under cold water. When the vegetables are turning golden, add the lentils, the turmeric and chilli powder and season generously with salt and pepper. Add the boiling water, bring to the boil and simmer for 10 minutes, stirring occasionally.

Cut the frankfurters into 1 cm (½ inch) lengths and add to the soup. Simmer for another 5 minutes before serving sprinkled with a little parsley.

SOUPS

21

Summer Tomato Soup ⓥ

Here is a kind of instant Gazpacho, that famous Spanish soup which is supposed to be based on garlic. There is a hint of garlic in this, but not that much, and the soup has the added advantage that it is equally good heated, if you prefer. It's important to note that I say heated not cooked, as the intention is to keep the freshness of the ingredients.

time

15 mins

Serves 4

225 g (8 oz) cherry tomatoes, halved
1 bunch spring onions, cut into 2.5 cm (1 inch) pieces
1 medium green pepper, seeded and quartered
½ teaspoon garlic purée
2 tablespoons olive oil
salt and freshly ground black pepper
600 ml (1 pint) tomato juice
1 tablespoon chopped fresh or frozen parsley, to garnish

Put all the vegetables, the garlic purée and olive oil into a food processor and chop until you have a medium fine purée. Season generously with salt and pepper before stirring into the chilled (or hot) tomato juice. Either way, serve immediately, sprinkled with the chopped parsley.

TOMATO JUICE

● This is a much undervalued ingredient, which we tend just to drink in small glasses as an aperitif. In fact it makes marvellous soups and adds enormous richness to tomato sauces.

● I rather favour it served at brunch, with a good mixture of flavourings including lemon juice, a shot or two of tabasco or chilli sauce, a little Worcestershire sauce and ½ teaspoon celery salt.

SOUPS

Tomato Juice
CRAFTY INGREDIENT

The area of salads is, perhaps, where the biggest advance has been made in recent years in terms of the resources that we have available. Supermarkets, in particular, have led this development by offering an extraordinary range of lettuces that vary from tiny, crisp, mini cos to fabulous loose-leafed oakleaf, that vary in colour from almost bright red to the deepest, darkest green and, what's more, they are available all year. In addition, tomatoes now come in an extraordinary range of sizes, shapes, flavours and even colours. There's spinach, watercress and rocket, all intended for salads, plus the more traditional ingredients such as celery, beetroot and spring onions. There are also a variety of dressings, although most of these can be improved at home with a little additional flavouring. Then, of course, there are the ready prepared packets, where different combinations of greenery and even dressings are arranged for you in advance.

The recipes for salads I've suggested here are really meant to be eaten as courses or dishes on their own rather than as accompaniments to a main dish, although one or two of them do work rather well in that way too. When you're making dressings, remember that good-quality ingredients show up more here than in any other dish, as there's no cooking applied to them. Good-quality oil, fresh lemon juice and real wine vinegar, all really make a substantial difference and, mixed properly, can produce the kind of dressing that people mop up off their plates with bread after the salad is finished.

SALADS

Pronto Pasta Salad

We tend to think of pasta as just a hot dish, and indeed in Italy it's usually eaten like that, but very often as part of the antipasti. *In fish restaurants, in particular, you find a delicious salad made from cold cooked pasta. You may want to do the same thing yourself and use one of the new quick cooking pastas which can be cooled and used within 10 minutes. Fish seems to be the ideal addition to a salad like this, although you may want to leave it out and just make a vegetarian version.*

time

15 mins

Serves 4

225 g (8 oz) 5 minute quick cooking pasta

2 teaspoons olive oil

juice of ½ lemon

4 tablespoons mayonnaise

salt and freshly ground black pepper

1 small head fennel, chopped

4 spring onions, chopped

225 g (8 oz) prawns, cooked and shelled

1 tablespoon chopped fresh or frozen fennel or dill, to garnish

Cook the pasta in a large saucepan of boiling water with a pinch of salt and 1 teaspoon of oil for 5 minutes. Drain in a colander and rinse under cold running water. When cold, stir in the remaining teaspoon of olive oil to stop the pasta sticking.

Mix the lemon juice into the mayonnaise, season and mix half of it with the fennel, onions and prawns. Mix the rest with the pasta. Arrange the pasta around the edge of a serving plate and fill the centre with the prawn and fennel mixture. If wished, chill in the fridge for 1–2 hours before serving. Serve garnished with the fennel or dill.

QUICK-COOKING PASTA

● This is a totally new technical development whereby dried pasta can be cooked in only 5 minutes. It's a great benefit halving the cooking time and it is achieved by introducing ridges to the inside of the pasta to allow it to absorb more heat and water. It comes in all sorts of shapes and sizes, though not yet, as far as I know, as spaghetti. Use it in exactly the same way as any pasta.

● It can be dressed with a sauce, used as a basis for a rich stew, or mixed with vegetables and cream sauce for a delicious gratin.

SALADS

Bitter Leafed Salad with Spiked Dressing Ⓥ

● These come in a variety of flavours including Blue Cheese, French and Thousand Island. All of them are interesting enough in their own right but I find they tend to be a little vinegary in flavour. The addition of a little extra good olive oil and a pinch of sugar alleviates this.

● The addition of herbs, garlic, chilli pepper, lemon peel, a tablespoon of tomato purée, (not all at once) all add different piquancies and balances to the basic ready made dressings.

The range of salad ingredients available at the moment is quite extraordinary. As well as the various lettuces to which we are accustomed, there are a number of bitter leaves, like rocket and radiccio, to add to our own traditional watercress and chicory. In addition there are a whole range of excellent dressings which are fine on their own but even nicer when they have a little something added to them. This salad will, of course, vary depending on the ingredients available to you. It can be eaten as a course on its own, with grilled meat or following a rich and substantial main course.

time

10 mins

Serves 4

1 large bag of mixed bitter salad leaves
(including some radiccio, sorrel or rocket)
1 bunch watercress
250 ml (8 fl oz) fresh French dressing
1 tablespoon olive oil
½ teaspoon sugar
2 teaspoons frozen Provençal herbs
(a mixture of basil, oregano and thyme)

Wash the salad leaves, according to the instructions on the packet, and add the watercress, divided into sprigs. Dry thoroughly in a salad dryer or tea-towel and put into a large salad bowl.

Pour half the dressing into a food processor, add the olive oil, sugar and herbs and blend until thoroughly mixed and homogenized. Pour the dressing over the salad, toss together thoroughly and serve.

French Dressing
CRAFTY INGREDIENT

SALADS

Grilled Goats' Cheese Salad

Grilled goats' cheese salad has become the ubiquitous first course in France. It's impossible to go to any restaurant, grand or small, and not find it. This is because it's both effortless to prepare and delicious to eat. Recently, there have been attempts to grill the salad on which the goats' cheese sits, not simply out of laziness but because the idea of grilled radiccio or frisée appeals. I'm afraid it doesn't to me, so I just place the cheese on a croûton on a bitter leaf salad.

time

10 mins

Serves 4

1 curly or bitter leafed lettuce, such as frisée, oak leaf or endive

4 slices French bread

Two 4 cm (1½ inch) goats' cheeses

FOR THE DRESSING:

2 tablespoons olive oil

4 tablespoons sunflower oil

1 tablespoon lemon juice

1 tablespoon red wine vinegar

1 teaspoon Dijon mustard

½ teaspoon salt

½ teaspoon sugar

Pre-heat the grill. Wash the lettuce, separating it into leaves, half the size of a postcard and dry thoroughly. Put the dressing ingredients in a blender or a jar with a well-fitting lid and blend together.

Grill the slices of French bread on one side only. Cut each cheese in half widthways and place on the untoasted sides of bread. Return to the grill and cook until the cheese is flecked with brown, bubbling on top and starting to melt.

Toss the lettuce leaves with the dressing and pile on to individual plates. Place the bubbling cheese croûtons in the centre and serve immediately.

SALADS

GOATS' CHEESE

● These little goats' cheese drums used to come exclusively from France but now they're widely produced in Britain, as well. They come in different flavours and ages. There are also varieties being produced, especially in Britain, with garlic and herbs. I find these unsuitable for this kind of salad although they are quite delicious eaten on their own at the end of a meal.

● The younger the cheese, the milder and creamier; as it gets older it gets drier and, normally, stronger-tasting.

Summary Salad Fried Rice Ⓥ

The idea for this recipe came to me one evening when faced with a bowl of uneaten rice and the ingredients for a salad. The salad seemed okay but incorporating the rice was a problem until I thought of doing it the other way round. This is therefore a Western version of a Chinese dish. It needs cooking and eating very quickly to get the benefit of the freshness of the salad ingredients. It's completely vegetarian and is nice enough on its own to make a light lunch or delicious snack. To make it more substantial, you can pre-cook a 2-egg omelette, cut it into slices and put it on top of the rice just before serving.

time

15 mins

Serves 4

225 g (8 oz) vine-ripened tomatoes

1 cos lettuce

½ cucumber

50 ml (2 fl oz) vegetable oil

4 spring onions, sliced into 5mm (¼ inch) pieces

½ teaspoon garlic purée

½ teaspoon ginger purée

1 tablespoon soy sauce

350 g (12 oz) cold cooked rice

Quarter the tomatoes or cut into 8 if they are very large. Slice the cos lettuce into 1 cm (½ inch) ribbons. Halve the cucumber lengthways, scoop out and discard the seeds and cut into thin half-moon shapes.

Heat the oil in a frying pan or wok and fry the spring onions with the garlic and ginger for about 30 seconds. Add the cucumber and tomatoes and toss and stir quickly. Add the soy sauce and let the mixture bubble for not more than 30 seconds. Stir in the lettuce and the rice and toss vigorously over a high heat for about 1–1½ minutes, until the mixture is well mixed, the rice is hot but the lettuce still bright emerald green. Serve immediately on plates or in Chinese bowls.

SALADS

28

VINE-RIPENED TOMATOES

● These are a new arrival in our shops, tomatoes actually ripened on the plant. While the varieties are no different from those it's been possible to buy for some time, the flavour is! This is because the sugars in the tomatoes have developed in a way that they simply don't when they're picked green and ripened in a ripening house or in one of the artificial atmospheres that are used to develop their colour. Make sure that the tomatoes you buy are still attached to the stems they were on as it's very difficult to ripen them other than on the plant itself.

● They're delicious of course in salads, but if you're going to cook them they need to be cooked extremely quickly and lightly. Grill them, sprinkled perhaps with a little Parmesan or Gruyère cheese, as they do in South-West France, or add at the last minute to a vegetable soup to add both freshness and sweetness.

Grilled Pears with Stilton and Walnuts

Here is a combination which is normally thought of as being after Christmas dinner flavours. The richness of the Stilton, the clarity of the pears and the crunchiness of the walnuts actually make a delicious salad and, in moderate quantities, because it's quite rich, a very interesting starter. Be careful with the grilling – it's meant to melt the cheese and warm the pears, not turn into a flambé – and don't use your best china!

time

15 mins

SHELLED WALNUTS

- The service that supermarkets, in particular, provide us with these days by supplying shelled nuts is of great value. I find it impossible, especially with walnuts, to shell enough to cook with, as I'm afraid I always eat them as I'm doing it.
- They're marvellous mixed into salads and very good with vegetables, especially vegetarian gratins.
- They make an excellent ingredient in various cakes, both as a part of the mixture and as an elegant and crunchy decoration.

Serves 4

4 thin slices crusty white bread, not pre-sliced
50 g (2 oz) butter
2 large, ripe pears
100 g (4 oz) Stilton cheese
50 g (2 oz) shelled walnut halves
sprigs of fresh parsley, to garnish

Pre-heat the grill, then lightly toast the bread slices on one side only. Generously butter the untoasted sides of bread, right up to the edges. Peel each pear, halve and core, then cut lengthways into thin slices. Fan the slices across the buttered side of the bread. Crumble the Stilton cheese and spread over the pears. Dot with the walnut halves.

Return to the grill until the cheese has melted and is bubbling and the walnuts are browned but not burnt. Serve immediately, garnished with parsley sprigs.

Walnuts
CRAFTY INGREDIENT

SALADS

Oz WINE The Cost of Wine

Wine prices have been fairly stable over the past decade. Despite rises in duty, not to forget a hike in VAT, you can still buy drinkable wine for £2.99. So, why bother to fork out £3.99…or £4.99…or even more?

There are numerous factors that influence wine prices, ranging from the quality of the grapes right through to the weight of the bottle, not to mention labour costs and variable exchange rates. Much also depends on the style of wine – oak-ageing, for instance, adds anything up to a pound to the production costs of a bottle. Technological advances and greater efficiency in both vineyard and winery have helped to drive costs down and the keen bargaining skills of wine buyers ensure that producers aren't too profit-greedy. However, some costs are more or less fixed. The Chancellor makes no distinction between, for example, non-vintage Liebfraumilch and 20 year-old Château Latour when he levies his duties and shipping costs are remarkably consistent regardless of distance.

So, for a £2.99 bottle, well over half of your money is immediately taken by the Exchequer. After the costs of shipping, packaging and other overheads, plus, of course, profit for winemaker and retailer, you've spent a staggering £2.54 on parts you can't drink and a mere 45p on the actual wine itself! As the chart below demonstrates, you only have to spend an extra pound to quite literally buy wine worth twice as much!

Key:
- Minimum fixed costs – duty, VAT, freight
- Other overheads – corks, bottles etc.
- Average total profit – grower, winemaker and retailer
- Cost of wine

£2.99: £1.57 · 25p · 72p · 45p

£3.99: £1.78 · 30p · £1.03 · 90p

£8.99: £2.58 · 50p · £2.44 · £3.47

Pâté used just to mean a large slice of what we might call a terrine – meat and liver minced together and baked. It still can mean that of course, and very nice some of them are too, but they do tend to take quite a while to prepare and cook. A whole range of other pâtés and potted foods now manage to perform exactly the same role, providing a substantial and strongly flavoured mixture to put on toast or biscuits or to eat with salads as a starter. Secondly, this new range of pâtés rarely need much cooking and are very easy to prepare. Many of them do not contain meat and there are several fish and vegetarian pâtés from different parts of the world.

Last but not least, there is a new highly flavoured range of fresh salsas from South America, originally intended as dips but which still fulfil the role of a strongly flavoured, spicy first course. I've included a couple of those here, as well as some fish versions, both hot and cold. Canned fish makes very good pâté and, indeed, is one of the few areas in which canning seems to be the best means of preserving food.

I've also made use of ready prepared shellfish, in this particular case crab, which I've turned into a hot starter. If you're looking for something more cooling, there is Hummus, a lovely golden chick pea pâté from the Middle East, and a very quick-to-make liver pâté.

PATES AND DIPS

Hot Crab with Sour Cream and Dijon Mustard

This is a luxury dish, although made much easier now by the readily available crab taken out of its shell. It's hard work otherwise. Crab goes particularly well with sour cream and the flavour of mustard is a traditional one to spike it. Serve this in individual ramekin dishes and have plenty of crisp, crusty French bread to mop up every last morsel of flavour.

time

30 mins

Serves 4

225 g (8 oz) dressed crab
  (white and brown crab meat separated)
1 tablespoon plain Dijon mustard
salt and freshly ground black pepper
125 ml (4 fl oz) sour cream
juice of 1 lemon
50 g (2 oz) Gruyère cheese, grated
French bread, to serve

Pre-heat the oven to 200°C/400°F/Gas 6.

Mix the brown meat of the crab with the Dijon mustard and season well with black pepper. Divide the mixture equally between four 2.5–4 cm (1–1½ inch) ramekin dishes and spread over the bottom of the dishes. Mix 3 tablespoons of the sour cream with the white crab meat and lemon juice. Spread equally over the brown crab meat. Mix the remaining sour cream with the grated cheese and lay on top of the dishes.

Stand the dishes on a baking tray and bake in the oven for 15–20 minutes, until the cheese is melted and bubbling and the crab mixture is hot. Serve with French bread.

DRESSED CRAB

● You can now buy dressed crab fresh or frozen. In my opinion the fresh is better but the frozen is often more widely available. Sometimes the dressed fresh is actually in the crab shell. It's a great luxury to have the work done for you with something as fiddly as crab.

● Make sure that, when you take the meat out of the shell, you keep the white and brown meat separate, as they have very different flavours and textures and often uses.

● The white meat makes a delicious addition to sweetcorn in a Chinese-style soup and the brown meat makes excellent potted crab mixed with half its weight of butter and a splash of chilli sauce.

PATES AND DIPS

Instant Tuna Pâté

One of the great ways of starting any meal is with a pâté. In recent years fish pâtés and terrines have become more and more fashionable, partly for health reasons and partly because they provide a lovely delicate way of eating fish even for those people who 'don't like it'. This tuna pâté is incredibly easy to make and needs no more than 15–20 minutes in the fridge, just to firm up before serving. It also has the advantage of being able to travel in its pot for picnics and other such outdoor occasions.

CANNED TUNA

● Canned tuna is one of the greatest store cupboard standbys. It comes in a variety of sizes and packs and is available in oil or brine. Brine is best for dishes that use the fish as a cooking ingredient and oil for those that use it cold.

● It's terrific in Salade Niçoise, makes an excellent filling for an omelette and a super, quickly cooked fish pie.

Serves 4

200g (7 oz) can tuna chunks in olive oil
1 tablespoon mayonnaise
2 teaspoons tomato ketchup
25 g (1 oz) butter, softened
juice of ½ lemon
salt and freshly ground black pepper
hot brown toast or crisp savoury biscuits, to serve

Put the tuna in a food processor with all the other ingredients and season with salt and pepper. Blend until smooth, scraping down the sides a few times to make sure all the ingredients are well mixed.

Turn the pâté into an attractive pottery serving bowl or individual ramekin dishes and place in the fridge for 20 minutes, until firm. If wished, the pâté can be stored in the fridge for up to 4 days if a little melted butter is poured over the top to seal and then covered with cling film.

Serve with brown toast or crisp savoury biscuits.

Tuna
CRAFTY INGREDIENT

PATES AND DIPS

Quick Hummus

Hummus is one of those dishes that's become almost universal. It began life, one suspects, as an ingredient in a Turkish menu but has spread all over the Middle East, to the Greek and Dalmatian coasts and, thanks to the Algerian influence, into southern France as well. It's basically a purée of chick peas but much improved by the addition of one or two other special ingredients. Traditionally, it's made by soaking the chick peas for six to twelve hours and then cooking them for another two. This recipe is really a much craftier way of achieving the same result. Hummus can be made from a coarse or fine purée. My preference is for the very fine version but that is a matter of taste.

time

5 mins

Serves 4

420 g (14 oz) can cooked chick peas
1 tablespoon tahini (sesame seed paste)
juice of 1 lemon
1 garlic clove
1 teaspoon salt
3 tablespoons olive oil
½ teaspoon chilli powder
½ teaspoon turmeric
salt and freshly ground black pepper
a pinch of paprika, to garnish

Drain the chick peas in a sieve and rinse well under cold water. Put the chick peas, tahini, lemon juice, garlic, salt and oil in a food processor and blend until smooth, adding a little water if necessary.

Stir in the chilli powder, turmeric, salt and pepper and pour the mixture into a serving bowl. Sprinkle the top with a pinch of paprika, to garnish.

TAHINI

● Tahini comes in jars and looks a bit like slightly grey honey. It's made from puréed sesame seeds and usually has a little oil floating on top. This can be stirred in to make the mixture coherent. It has a flavour that's reminiscent of peanut butter but more subtle and gentle.
● In the Middle East it's mixed with natural yoghurt and used as a sauce for fish.

PATES AND DIPS

Crafty Liver Pâté

This is one of the first things I ever learnt to make, and as a dinner party standby it has no equal. It's an instant home-made pâté which begins as liver sausage. As with so many of these sorts of dishes, however, the quality of the liver sausage is crucial. I favour the calf's liver sausage that you find in good delicatessens and kosher speciality shops. I ought to add that the mixture isn't kosher when you've finished, as dairy and meat products are mixed together. Hot crisp toast, and plenty of it, little gherkins and some French mustard are ideal accompaniments.

time

25 mins

Serves 4

250 g (9 oz) good-quality liver sausage
75 g (3 oz) unsalted butter
½ teaspoon garlic salt
½ teaspoon celery salt
hot toast, to serve

Remove the skin of the liver sausage and mash the sausage thoroughly with a fork. Melt the butter, add the garlic salt and celery salt and stir until dissolved. Stir into the liver sausage and mix well together.

Pack the mixture into individual dishes or 1 large dish and chill in the freezer for 20 minutes before serving with hot toast.

● These are speciality sausages found on the delicatessen counter. They can just be sliced and eaten with a selection of other cold meats, but they're also excellent mixed into salads, particularly rice or pasta salads, and finely diced and added to omelettes.

Luncheon and Liver Sausages
CRAFTY INGREDIENT

PATES AND DIPS

Lemon Sardines

This is a dish from the sixties, when bistros were fashionable and candles were stuck in wine bottles. It's still, however, a nice idea to serve a very strong-flavoured fish pâté in hollowed-out lemons. They make an ideal individual serving and add visual pleasure as well as flavour to the dish. You can place them in individual egg cups if you like. An egg spoon is ideal for getting the pâté out of the lemon shells.

time

25 mins

Serves 4

4 medium thin-skinned lemons

Two 120 g (4½ oz) cans sardines in olive oil

2 teaspoons chopped frozen or fresh chives

2 teaspoons tomato purée

1 teaspoon freshly ground black pepper

½ teaspoon chilli purée or sauce

fingers of hot brown toast, to serve

Cut 1 cm (½ inch) off the stalk end of each lemon and reserve. Using a sharp knife or grapefruit knife, cut inside the lemons to remove the centres. Put the lemon pulp and juice into a bowl and reserve.

In a separate bowl, mash the sardines, including the oil, and all the other ingredients, adding about 2 teaspoons of the lemon juice and pulp to the mixture. Mash with a fork until smooth and well mixed, then pack the mixture back into the empty lemon shells. Top with the reserved caps and chill in the fridge for 15–20 minutes before serving with fingers of hot brown toast.

CANNED SARDINES

● Sardines are so highly prized in France that they are sold in the most expensive gourmet shops in cans about twice the size of those we're used to buying in this country. They are laid down rather like wine, being turned every year to ensure that the flavour spreads equally. I have to say that, although I've tasted sardines treated like this, they taste no better to me than the best olive oil canned sardines.

● They are quite delicious on their own with brown bread and butter and a squeeze of lemon over them or as part of a mixed hors d'oeuvre with radishes, olives, a grated carrot salad and a tomato salad.

● They are a wonderful standby for the lunch box, mashed and flavoured, as in this recipe, and used in sandwiches.

PATES AND DIPS

CHILLI PUREE
OR SAUCE

● Chilli purée comes in several varieties. One is fresh puréed chillies with nothing but a little salt added to keep them fresh. This indicates that chillies not only have pungency but also flavour. The mixture also comes in green and red forms and is an excellent ingredient in any dish requiring chillies.

● Use it for Mexican dishes like *Quick Chilli Con Carne*, (see p. 79). Indian curries and South- East Asian food, particularly Thai food which uses a lot of chilli. I like it stirred into a little tomato ketchup and eaten with *Scrambled Chilli Eggs* (see p. 74).

● Chilli sauce comes in all sorts of varieties, from the very thin, pungent Tabasco to the rather thicker, sweeter Malaysian-style sauces which look, but don't taste, like tomato ketchup.

Crafty Killing Salsa Ⓥ

Salsas are the uncooked Mexican sauces which have become so popular in a variety of forms. Traditionally, they were used as condiments on the table with Mexican or South American meals. We've come to use them as dips or even vegetarian pâtés to be used on crisps or corn chips or as an addition to an exotic hors d'oeuvre. This salsa is punishingly, deliciously hot.

time

5 mins

Serves 4

I large red pepper, seeded and chopped

3 medium tomatoes, quartered

I medium purple skinned or ordinary onion, cut into 8

I tablespoon chilli purée or sauce

2 tablespoons salad oil

I tablespoon red wine vinegar

pinch of sugar

I tablespoon tomato purée

I teaspoon chopped fresh or frozen parsley

Depending on the texture you want, either roughly chop all the ingredients, except the parsley, or purée them in a food processor until you get a well blended but slightly grainy texture.

Put the mixture into an attractive rustic bowl and stir in the parsley. Covered, this will keep in the fridge for up to 24 hours.

PATES AND DIPS

Chilli Purée
CRAFTY INGREDIENT

37

Cooling Green Salsa

This recipe is not only an alternative to but may even be a remedy for its cousin, the Crafty Killing Salsa (see p. 37). It's green and quite gentle although it has a little pungency from the mixture of herbs and other ingredients. Cooling and refreshing, it is in the style of a guacamole.

time

5 mins

Serves 4

1 ripe avocado

1 bunch prepared spring onions, cut into 2 cm (¾ inch) pieces

1 small green pepper, seeded and chopped

2 tablespoons salad oil

1 tablespoon white wine vinegar

juice of ½ lemon

pinch of salt

pinch of sugar

2 tablespoons chopped fresh or frozen coriander

Cut the avocado in half, and depending how soft it is, either finely chop or mix it with all the remaining ingredients. Depending on the texture you prefer, you can either finely chop the ingredients by hand or put all the ingredients into a food processor and blend until mixture is creamy but still has some texture and flecks of colour from the other ingredients to it. Add all the remaining ingredients and blend to form a purée. Once the mixture is roughly chopped, scrape down the sides and blend again for another 5–10 seconds. The mixture should be quite creamy from the avocado but still have some texture and flecks of colour from the other ingredients.

Pour the mixture into a serving bowl. The salsa will keep for 2–3 hours if sprinkled with some more lemon juice to prevent discolouring and covered with cling film.

PREPARED SPRING ONIONS

● It may seem crazy to buy ready prepared vegetables when it only takes a minute or two to prepare each of them, but that can add up to half an hour's work before a meal. Therefore, when I'm pressed for time I'm very happy to buy prepared vegetables, including spring onions.

● When you do buy prepared spring onions it's worth making sure that they've been recently trimmed and there's no sign of browning around the edges.

● They can be used in all the ways spring onions are normally used such as in salads and chopped into soups or vegetable dishes.

PATES AND DIPS

38

Spring Onions

CRAFTY INGREDIENT

Over the last few years, so the researchers tell us, pizza has become the most popular dish on earth. I'm not sure if the researchers actually spent much time in the Chinese or Indian interiors before they came to this conclusion, but I'm willing to accept it for all those places where pizza is an option. Needless to say, it's not Italian pizza that's made these incredible strides but the American fast food versions. Every supermarket today is crammed with countless varieties of pizza. I'm sorry to say that the researchers also suggest that pizzas which include pineapple chunks are the most popular. You won't find any of these here but you will find a number of instant pizza recipes using both pizza bases and French bread. There are also some recipes, from the Mediterranean and India, using breads as a basis for other dishes.

Finally, it's worth looking at the amazing range of ready-to-use pastry products that are now available. These range from ready-made pastry which you can roll out yourself, ready rolled pastry and pastry mixes through to pre-baked pastry shells, both sweet and savoury. I have also recently come across wholemeal pastry which already has herbs in it to add extra flavour. These choices are unbelievably useful for crafty cooking.

Quick Cheese and Spinach Tart

Quiches have gone out of fashion in posh restaurants but everyone I know seems to really enjoy this cheese and spinach version. If you don't like spinach, you could substitute thinly sliced, quick-fried courgettes or even a thinly sliced onion, also quick-fried. This is a tart best served hot and bubbling.

time

30 mins

Serves 4

150 g (5 oz) frozen spinach
1 teaspoon chilli sauce
2 eggs, separated
300 g (11 oz) tub cheese sauce
20 cm (8 inch) pre-baked savoury pastry shell
25 g (1 oz) freshly grated Parmesan cheese

Pre-heat the oven to 200°C/400°F/Gas 6.

Put the spinach into a non-stick saucepan and heat gently until it thaws and is smooth, stirring frequently. Mix the chilli sauce and the egg yolks into the cheese sauce and stir until smooth. Stir into the spinach mixture and heat gently until just below boiling point. Remove from the heat.

Whisk the egg whites until stiff, then fold into the spinach mixture. Pour the mixture into the pastry shell and sprinkle with the Parmesan cheese.

Bake in the oven for 20–25 minutes, until the mixture has risen and has turned golden brown. It will sink a little as it comes out of the oven but should be eaten warm.

● All supermarkets and many bakery stores now sell these ready prepared in both sweet and savoury form. The savoury ones make marvellous instant quiches and the sweet ones can be used as a basis for dishes such as custard tarts.

● Finely chopped Ratatouille poured into a warmed pastry shell makes a marvellous Tarte Provençale, especially if you beat 1–2 eggs, pour them over the top and flash the tart under the grill until they set.

Pie Shells

CRAFTY INGREDIENT

PIZZAS, PITTAS AND SNACKS

Tomato and Cheese Pizza

Pizzas are one of the favourite foods of the decade, for both adults and children. Here are three quick ones – all very different but all authentic in taste.

They use very different bases, both the traditional round ones and the modern French bread ones. The secret with any pizza is a really hot oven so don't be tempted to cook it in anything other than a pre-heated one.

time

20 mins

Makes one 23 cm (9 inch) pizza

23 cm (9 inch) ready-to-bake pizza base
1 teaspoon garlic purée
1 tablespoon sun-dried tomato purée
3–4 tablespoons bottled fresh chopped tomato sauce
100 g (4 oz) Mozzarella cheese, grated
1 teaspoon frozen basil
1 teaspoon frozen oregano
1–2 tablespoons lemon-flavoured olive oil (see p. 44)

Pre-heat the oven to 220°C/425°F/Gas 7.

Place the pizza base on a baking tray and spread the base with the garlic and sun-dried tomato purée. Spoon on the tomato sauce and spread over the pizza, leaving a clean rim around the edge. Sprinkle over the cheese and herbs and drizzle with the olive oil.

Bake in the oven for about 12 –15 minutes, until golden brown.

READY-MADE PIZZA BASES

● Ready-made pizza bases come in a variety of styles which include fresh, chilled and frozen and thick and thin. It's best to look for ones that aren't too thick as these can be rather doughy. I also avoid unusual ones like wholemeal or herb flavoured as I prefer to put the flavourings on to the base myself.

● Yeast-risen bases seem to provide the crispiest results.

● A good pizza base can also just be sprinkled with olive oil and salt and spread with a little garlic purée to produce a focaccia -style pizza bread.

PIZZAS, PITTAS AND SNACKS

Seafood Pizza

There are many variations on pizza toppings and not all include cheese, such as this fishy version.

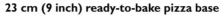

ANCHOVY FILLETS

● Anchovy fillets are sold in small oblong tins in olive oil. They look like small dark brown strips and may need separating as they come out of the tin as they are usually quite tightly packed in.

● Anchovy fillets have many other uses apart from being included in pizza toppings. They add a punch to salads, especially tomato salads, are a flavoursome addition to sandwiches and a mandatory ingredient in caesar salads. In days gone by, anchovies were often added to beef or game stews, to add pungency, but surprisingly not a fishy taste. It's a trick worth trying.

Serves 4

23 cm (9 inch) ready-to-bake pizza base
2 tablespoons garlic-flavoured olive oil (see p. 44)
6 tablespoons bottled fresh chopped Italian tomato sauce
200 g (7 oz) can tuna in oil
1 tablespoon chopped fresh dill or fennel leaves
6 anchovy fillets
7 black olives, pitted

Pre-heat the oven to 220°C/425°F/Gas 7.

Place the pizza base on a baking tray and pour 1 tablespoon of the garlic oil over the pizza. Spread the tomato sauce over the base, leaving a clear rim around the edge. Put the tuna in a bowl and break into flakes, stir in the chopped herbs, then sprinkle over the pizza. Arrange the anchovies, like the spokes of a wheel, to top, dot an olive between each and place the last in the centre. Drizzle over the remaining oil.

Bake in the oven for about 12 minutes, until golden brown.

Anchovy Fillets
CRAFTY INGREDIENT

PIZZAS, PITTAS AND SNACKS

Double Cheese and Mushroom Pizza

This topping can also be added to a ready-to-bake pizza base but for this recipe a short stick of French bread, the wider the better, is what you need.

time

20 mins

Serves 4

1 small stick of French bread, cut in half lengthways

175 g (6 oz) Gorgonzola cheese

25 g (1 oz) butter

175 g (6 oz) chestnut mushrooms, finely sliced

50 g (2 oz) freshly grated Parmesan cheese

2 teaspoons frozen garlic granules or 1 large garlic clove, finely chopped

1 teaspoon frozen thyme

2 tablespoons olive oil (preferably truffle-flavoured)

Pre-heat the grill. In a bowl, mash together the Gorgonzola cheese and butter, then spread it over the bread halves. Arrange the sliced mushrooms in neat overlapping layers over the top. Sprinkle over the Parmesan cheese, garlic and thyme and drizzle over the oil.

Place on a baking tray and grill until the cheese is bubbling and the bread begins to brown.

PIZZAS, PITTAS AND SNACKS

FLAVOURED OLIVE OIL

● As well as the enormous range of olive oils that you can buy today, there are a number of interesting flavoured ones.
● Truffle oil, which is flavoured with the most expensive mushrooms in the world, produces a lovely, rich, earthy, mushroom flavour and, not surprisingly, is the most expensive. Other good oils to look out for are lemon and garlic, both of which are nice in salad dressings.
● The garlic-flavoured variety is good added to *Quick Italian Bean Soup* (see p. 20)

Olive Oil

CRAFTY INGREDIENT

Pitta Bread
CRAFTY INGREDIENT

PITTA BREAD

● Pitta breads have spread effortlessly across Britain in the wake of the doner kebab shops. They are tremendous for putting in grilled lamb, in its various forms, but they're used for other things too. They come in a variety of shapes, sizes and flavours these days – small (mini), round and wholemeal. I've even seen herb and garlic varieties. They're excellent for just putting salad in for serving on their own or as a lighter accompaniment to another kind of grill or dish.

● The mini ones are loved by children, particularly if you put in colourful ingredients.

● They're nice too for containing stews but make sure not to add too much liquid.

● I always eat them hot and they're very good cut into strips, buttered and eaten with honey, as they do in Greece.

Greek Lamb Kebabs in Pitta

The trick with kebabs is to buy lamb that's prepared and boned in advance.

time

30 mins

Serves 4

450 g (1 lb) lamb neck fillet
½–1 teaspoon garlic purée
2 tablespoons olive oil
2 tablespoons lemon juice
1 teaspoon chopped fresh or frozen thyme
1 teaspoon chopped fresh or frozen oregano
1 small cos lettuce
2 medium tomatoes
100 ml (3½ fl oz) Greek natural yoghurt
½ teaspoon salt (optional)
4 large pitta breads

Pre-heat the grill. Cut the lamb fillets in half lengthways and 3–4 times widthways, making 2 cm (¾ inch) cubes of lamb. Put these in a bowl with 1 teaspoon garlic purée, the oil and lemon juice and stir thoroughly. Add the herbs and leave to marinate for 10–15 minutes.

Thread 6–8 pieces of lamb on flat metal skewers, packing them close together towards the sharp end of the skewer and leaving plenty of cool handle sticking out. Cook under the grill for about 15 minutes, turning every 5 minutes, until crisp on the outside but still juicy on the inside.

Meanwhile, shred the lettuce and thinly slice the tomatoes. If you like garlic, stir the extra ½ teaspoon garlic purée into the Greek yoghurt. If not, stir in the ½ teaspoon salt. In the last 5 minutes of grilling, add the pitta breads to the grill and allow to warm through on both sides.

Lay the pitta breads on a board and trim 5 mm (¼ inch) round one side of each, allowing the breads to open into an envelope or pocket. Place a quarter of the chopped lettuce in the cavity, slide in a skewer of lamb and, keeping the lamb inside the pocket, remove the skewer. Top with the tomatoes and yoghurt sauce, and serve.

PIZZAS, PITTAS AND SNACKS

Sizzling Turkey Fajitas

Turkeys and tortillas and the sauce that brings them together all come from Mexico, although this kind of cooking tends to come from the North of Mexico and is much influenced by Texas-style food. Texan food is, however, influenced by Mexico as well, so I think it's as genuine a form of cooking as you can get outside the deep jungles of the Yucatan Peninsula. This is really easy food but quite delicious and very moreish. I never seem to make quite enough of it. The sauce usually comes in jars that has too much for one serving so that solves that problem. It is fabulous food for barbecues.

time

20 mins

Serves 4

> 1 tablespoon cooking oil
> 450 g (1 lb) stir-fry turkey strips
> 1 medium onion, sliced
> 1 green pepper, sliced
> 120 g (4 oz) jar Mexican enchilada or fajita sauce
> 1 packet of 8 soft tortillas
> 150 ml (5 fl oz) sour cream

Pre-heat the oven to 180°C/350°F/Gas 4.

    Heat the oil in a frying pan, add the turkey strips, making sure that they are all about the same size, and fry for 3–4 minutes, until they start to turn golden brown. Stir in the sliced onion and fry for 2–3 minutes, then add the green pepper and cook for a further 2–3 minutes. Add most of the Mexican sauce (depending on what the label says, this can be anything from mild to astonishingly hot, and it's entirely up to your taste). Bring to the boil and simmer for 5 minutes.

    Meanwhile, place the tortillas on a baking tray and warm in the oven for 5 minutes.

    To serve, put a tortilla on a plate, add some sauce, top with sour cream and roll the whole mixture up. It can be eaten with a knife or fork or, more authentically but more messily with the fingers.

PIZZAS, PITTAS AND SNACKS

MEXICAN SAUCES

● In recent years a number of British companies, as well as American ones, have begun to market a range of excellent Mexican sauces. They have unusual names depending on the specific dish for which they are intended. Burrito, enchilada and mesquite are just some of them, the latter tending to be a smoky flavoured sauce.

● Despite the labels, I find these sauces really only vary in their level of pungency and chilli heat. It's that which I look for in a variety of dishes, including Mexican-flavoured stir-fries with chicken, lamb, beef or turkey.

Punjabi Chicken Sandwich

This favourite picnic recipe of mine was inspired by an account by Elizabeth David of an Indian colonel's recipe. It is an excellent way of making an unexpectedly tasty sandwich that travels wonderfully.

time

20 mins

Serves 4

2 boneless chicken breasts, skinned

I tablespoon mild curry paste

10 cm (4 inch) piece of cucumber, grated

100 ml (3½ fl oz) natural yoghurt

pinch of salt

I French bread, measuring about 45 cm (18 inches)

3 tablespoons mango chutney

Pre-heat the grill. Rub the chicken breasts with the curry paste, then cook under the grill for 5–8 minutes on each side until tender.

Meanwhile, mix together the grated cucumber, the yoghurt and a pinch of salt. Cut the bread in half lengthways and remove some of the central white crumbs. Spread the bottom half with the yoghurt mixture, making sure that all the bread is covered. Spread the top half of bread with the mango chutney.

When the chicken breasts are cooked, slice them widthways into I cm (½) inch slices. Lay the slices on top of the yoghurt mixture. Place the top half of bread on top and press down gently. Wrap the bread in cling film.

When ready to eat, slice the bread into 5 cm (2 inch) lengths and serve, still wrapped in cling film, with a napkin. You remove the cling film as you eat the sandwich.

PIZZAS, PITTAS AND SNACKS

MANGO CHUTNEY

● The wonderful variety of mango chutneys that are now available make it worth experimenting with in almost every spicy dish. It comes in pure smooth forms, with great chunks of mango, with spices and additional flavours such as lime and ginger.

● As well as its obvious uses, I like it mixed into yoghurt as a dip, finely chopped as an ingredient in an exotic cream sauce for firm fish and, not least, mixed with a little Stilton cheese and spread on steak before grilling it.

Tapenade Rolls

Tapenade Rolls, Prawn Puffs (see p. 50) and Ratatouille Barquettes (see p. 50) are all nibbles are intended to be served with drinks at a cocktail party or before dinner. They're easy to make, quite impressive to look at and they make use of a variety of ready prepared ingredients that are found in all food stores and supermarkets these days. While they can be made in advance, none of them benefit from being frozen as some of the ingredients will have been frozen beforehand. They're therefore best made in the afternoon and eaten in the evening.

Prawn Puffs (see p. 50) and Ratatouille Barquettes (see p. 50)

time

25 mins

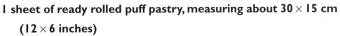

Makes about 25

I sheet of ready rolled puff pastry, measuring about 30 × 15 cm
   (12 × 6 inches)
4 tablespoons tapenade or olive purée mixture
I tablespoon mixed chopped fresh or frozen Provençal herbs,
   such as thyme, basil and oregano
I egg yolk, beaten

Pre-heat the oven to 220°C/425°F/Gas 7.

   Lay the sheet of puff pastry on a work surface and spread over the tapenade mixture to within 5 mm (¼ inch) of the edges. Sprinkle over the herbs and roll up lengthways like a Swiss roll. Cut into 1 cm (½ inch) slices and place on a dampened baking tray, cut side down. Bake in the oven for 10–15 minutes, until golden brown.

**PREPARED
PUFF PASTRY**

● Prepared puff pastry now comes in blocks, sheets and rings, vol-au-vent cases and decorative shapes. It's a blessing, as puff pastry is really hard work to prepare from scratch. I use it on all sorts of pies and pastries both sweet and savoury. I always keep some in the freezer, as it only takes an hour to thaw ready for use.

Puff Pastry
CRAFTY INGREDIENT

PIZZAS, PITTAS AND SNACKS

Prawn Puffs

time

20 mins

Makes 12

12 mini puff pastry vol-au-vent cases

100 g (4 oz) frozen shelled small prawns, thawed

2 teaspoons chopped fresh or frozen dill

2 tablespoons mayonnaise

juice of 1 lemon

Pre-heat the oven according to the instructions on the vol-au-vent packet. Place the cases on a baking tray and bake as directed.

Meanwhile, roughly chop the prawns and mix with the dill, mayonnaise and lemon juice until smooth. When the vol-au-vents are cooked, remove the tops and fill with the mixture. Serve hot or warm.

Ratatouille Barquettes

time

10 mins

Makes 10–12 or 24 (depending on the size of the cases)

1 small courgette, roughly sliced

2 medium tomatoes, halved

1 green pepper, seeded and roughly chopped

3 spring onions, roughly sliced

2 tablespoons olive oil

pinch of garlic salt

freshly ground black pepper

1 packet 2–4 cm (¾–1½ inches) barquette cases

pinch of chopped fresh or frozen oregano, to garnish

Chop the vegetables in a food processor until about the size of rice grains. Heat the oil, add the chopped vegetables and fry gently for 6–8 minutes, until just tender. Season with garlic salt and pepper. Allow to cool slightly, then use to fill the pastry cases. Sprinkle with oregano and serve warm or cold.

Oz's Dream Dozen

ASDA

WHITES

ASDA Vinho Verde *(Portugal)*   **Good Buy**

Frascati Superiore, Colli di Catone *(Italy)*

    Good Buy

ASDA Niersteiner Spiegelberg Kabinett

    (Germany)   **Good Buy**

Hardy's Nottage Hill Chardonnay *(Australia)*

    Mid-price

ASDA Chablis *(France)*   **Treat!**

REDS

ASDA South Australian Cabernet Sauvignon

    Good Buy

ASDA Chilean Cabernet Sauvignon-Merlot

    Good Buy

Beaujolais-Villages, Domaine de la Ronzes

    (France)   **Mid-price**

Hardy's Bankside Shiraz *(Australia)*   **Treat!**

Baron de Ley, Rioja Reserva *(Spain)*   **Treat!**

SPARKLING

ASDA Cava *(Spain)*   **Good Buy**

FORTIFIED

Stanton & Killeen Liqueur Muscat *(Australia)*

    Treat!

CO-OP (CWS)

WHITES

Co-op English Table Wine   **Good Buy**

Long Slim Chardonnay-Sémillon *(Chile)*

    Good Buy

Forster Schnepfenflug Riesling Kabinett

    (Germany)   **Mid-price**

Mâcon-Viré, Cave de Viré *(France)*   **Mid-price**

Glen Ellen Chardonnay *(California)*   **Treat!**

REDS

Long Mountain Cabernet Sauvignon

    (South Africa)   **Good Buy**

Co-op Californian Premium Red   **Good Buy**

Vine Vale Shiraz *(Australia)*   **Mid-price**

Château Reynella Cabernet Sauvignon-Merlot

    (Australia)   **Treat!**

Raimat Cabernet Sauvignon *(Spain)*   **Treat!**

SPARKLING

Marino Cava del Mediterraneo *(Spain)*

    Good Buy

FORTIFIED

Co-op Late Bottled Vintage Port   **Good Buy**

MARKS & SPENCER

WHITES

St Michael Country Chenin Blanc *(South Africa)*

    Good Buy

St Michael Italian White Table Wine   **Good Buy**

St Michael Casa Leone Chardonnay *(Chile)*

    Mid-price

St Michael Domaine Mandeville Chardonnay

    (France)   **Mid-price**

St Michael Rosemount Estate Hunter Valley

    Chardonnay *(Australia)*   **Treat!**

REDS

St Michael Bulgarian Cabernet Sauvignon

      Good Buy

St Michael Montepulciano d'Abruzzo *(Italy)*

      Good Buy

St Michael Fitou *(France)*   **Mid-price**

St Michael Chilean Cabernet Sauvignon

      Mid-price

St Michael Rioja *(Spain)*   **Treat!**

SPARKLING

St Michael Oudinot Brut Champagne **Treat!**

FORTIFIED

St Michael Fino Sherry   **Mid-price**

SAFEWAY

WHITES

Safeway Matra Mountain Oaked Chardonnay

    (Hungary)   **Good Buy**

Safeway Pinot Grigio delle Venezie *(Italy)*

      Mid-price

Montana Marlborough Sauvignon Blanc

    (New Zealand)   **Treat!**

Safeway Australian Oaked Chardonnay **Treat!**

Safeway Chablis, Cuvée Domaine Yvon Pautré

    (France)   **Treat!**

REDS

Safeway Romanian Pinot Noir Special Reserve

      Good Buy

Safeway Young Vatted Tempranillo *(Spain)*

      Good Buy

Safeway Domaine Vieux Manoir de Maransan,

    Côtes-du-Rhône *(France)*   **Mid-price**

Safeway Cabernet Sauvignon, Vin de Pays d'Oc

    (France)   **Mid-price**

Safeway Australian Oaked Shiraz   **Treat!**

SPARKLING

Safeway Sparkling Australian   **Good Buy**

FORTIFIED

Safeway LBV Port   **Mid-price**

SAINBURY'S

WHITES

Sainsbury's Australian Chardonnay **Good Buy**

Chapel Hill Chardonnay *(Hungary)* **Good Buy**

Sainsbury's Chilean Chardonnay **Mid-price**

La Baume Sauvignon Blanc, Vin de Pays d'Oc

    (France)   **Mid-price**

Château Carsin, Bordeaux Blanc *(France)* **Treat!**

REDS

Sainsbury's Jumilla *(Spain)*   **Good Buy**

Sainsbury's Cahors *(France)*   **Good Buy**

Sainsbury's Chilean Merlot, San Fernando

      Mid-price

Sainsbury's Copertino Riserva *(Italy)* **Mid-price**

Corbières La Voulte-Gasparet *(France)* **Treat!**

SPARKLING

Sainsbury's Champagne Extra Dry **Good Buy**

FORTIFIED

Sainsbury's Palo Cortado Sherry   **Treat!**

SOMERFIELD

WHITES

Haut-Poitou Sauvignon Blanc *(France)*

      Good Buy

Bairrada Branco *(Portugal)*   **Good Buy**

Morio Muskat St. Ursula *(Germany)* **Good Buy**

James Herrick Chardonnay, Vin de Pays d'Oc
(France) **Mid-price**

Gewürztraminer d'Alsace, Caves de Türckheim
(France) **Mid-price**

REDS

Somerfield Valencia Red *(Spain)* **Good Buy**

Somerfield Côtes-du-Rhône *(France)* **Good Buy**

I Grilli di Villi Thalia, Calatrasi *(Italy)* **Good Buy**

Penfolds Koonunga Hill Shiraz-Cabernet
Sauvignon *(Australia)* **Mid-price**

Château de Caraguilhes, Corbières *(France)*
Mid-price

SPARKLING

Seppelt Great Western Brut Reserve *(Australia)*
Good Buy

FORTIFIED

Somerfield Manzanilla Sherry, Gonzales Byass
Good Buy

TESCO

WHITES

Tesco Saumur *(France)* **Good Buy**

Wiltinger Scharzberg Riesling Kabinett
(Germany) **Good Buy**

Torres Viña Sol *(Spain)* **Mid-price**

Jacob's Creek Sémillon-Chardonnay *(Australia)*
Mid-price

Errázuriz Chardonnay *(Chile)* **Treat!**

REDS

Señorio de los Llanos, Valdepeñas *(Spain)*
Good Buy

Tesco Beyers Truter Pinotage *(South Africa)*
Mid-price

Salice Salentino *(Italy)* **Mid-price**

Beaujolais-Villages, Duboeuf *(France)* **Mid-price**

Chapel Hill Shiraz *(Australia)* **Treat!**

SPARKLING

Heemskerk Jansz Tasmanian Sparkling *(Australia)*
Mid-price

FORTIFIED

Mick Morris Liqueur Muscat *(Australia)*
Mid-price

WAITROSE

WHITES

Domaine de Planterieu, Vin de Pays des Côtes
de Gascogne *(France)* **Good Buy**

Oxford Landing Chardonnay *(Australia)*
Mid-price

Cook's Hawkes Bay Chardonnay
(New Zealand) **Mid-price**

Isla Negra Chardonnay *(Chile)* **Mid-price**

Chablis la Chablisiènne *(France)* **Treat!**

REDS

Winter Hill, Vin de Pays de l'Aude *(France)*
Good Buy

Don Hugo *(Spain)* **Good Buy**

Waitrose Good Ordinary Claret *(France)*
Mid-price

Avontuur Pinotage, Stellenbosch *(South Africa)*
Mid-price

Château Reynella Basket Pressed Shiraz
(Australia) **Treat!**

SPARKLING

Waitrose Cava Brut *(Spain)* **Good Buy**

FORTIFIED

Passito di Pantelleria, Pellegrino *(Italy)* **Treat!**

LIGHT MEALS